THE LITTLE STRAY CAT

Pictures by Sally Holmes

COLLINS COLOUR CUBS

There was once a stray cat without a name. She had once belonged to a family, but they had moved away, and hadn't taken her with them. So after she had stayed around the empty house for some time, she left it, and went to the woods.

She was sad, because she had liked belonging to a family. It was nice to lap milk from her own blue saucer. It was lovely to nibble at a fishhead, put down in her dish. It was delicious to wash herself in front of the warm kitchen fire, and it was fun to curl up in her own basket, and to feel somebody stroking her.

Now she had nobody. She lived in the woods and looked after herself. She made herself a kind of hidey-hole in a tree, and at night-time she came out to hunt rats and mice and rabbits.

But it was very lonely without anyone to love her. Sometimes the little stray used to

listen for children who came picnicking in the woods. Then she would pop her head out of the hole in the tree and wonder if she should jump down and go to them. Perhaps one of them might take her home and love her! But she never liked to jump down in case one of the children had a dog.

One day a little boy called Bob came through the woods alone. He was looking for toadstools to take to school, because the teacher was going to give a lesson on them.

The little boy had looked up into the tree where the stray had her hole. He saw a queer fungus growing out of the trunk, shaped like a saddle. "Well, that's not a toadstool, but I'm sure it belongs to the same family," said Bob, and he climbed up to get it. When he came near to the hole in the tree, he stared in surprise.

Two big green eyes were looking up at him out of the hole!

Then there came a soft purring noise, and Bob smiled. "A stray cat! Poor thing! It's living in a tree!"

He put down his hand and stroked the stray cat. She purred more loudly, and came right out.

"Oh, you're a tabby!" said Bob. "I like tabbies. What a nice soft little thing you are!"

He stroked the stray and made such a fuss of her that she quite lost her heart to Bob.

When he climbed down the tree, she climbed down too. When he ran through the wood, she ran behind him. When he turned to go home, she went with him.

She went right to the front door of his home. His mother was surprised to see the little tabby.

"Mother, it's a stray cat. I found her in a hole in a tree," said Bob. "She came all the way home with me. Can we keep her?"

"Oh, no, dear," said his mother. "I don't want a cat. Give her some milk and let her go."

Bob put her down a saucer of milk and the tabby lapped it up eagerly. She hadn't tasted milk for weeks! It was delicious.

"Now you must go," said Bob's mother and shooed the tabby away. She ran down the path, and looked back. What a pity she couldn't live with that nice boy, and belong to him!

She made up her mind that she would live near him. She wouldn't go back to the woods again. She would find a hole in a tree, quite near the house, and she would live there. She could catch mice and rats for her dinner. Perhaps just sometimes the boy would give her a little milk to drink.

The tabby hunted around for a good hole in a tree. Soon she found one in a big ash tree near the house. The tree was hollow inside, though it looked good enough outside. The cat made itself a comfortable hidey-hole and slept there whenever it wanted to.

It watched for Bob all the time. As soon as he appeared at the door, ready to go to school, the tabby jumped down from her tree and ran to him. She rubbed herself against his legs and purred loudly. It was so nice to have someone to love. What was the use of living if you couldn't love someone and have someone love you?

Bob loved the little cat and wished and wished that his mother would let him have her. But she shook her head every time he asked her, and at last got cross.

"You know quite well that when I say no, I mean no," she said. "Don't ask me again, please. It's quite a nice little cat, but I wish it wouldn't hang about the house so much. I hope it isn't a thief. If I catch it stealing the

fish or the milk I shall give it such a smacking that it will never come near again!"

"Mother, the tabby isn't a thief," said Bob. "*I* think she's a great help, because she catches so many rats and mice."

Each night Bob slept in his little bedroom, and each night the tabby slept in her hole in the big ash tree that overlooked the window. Sometimes when she popped her head out, she could see Bob standing at his window.

One night the wind got up and a terrible gale blew. It howled in the wood and bent the trees almost in half. It shouted round the house, and blew a chimney-pot off down the road. It blew the clouds to rags in the sky.

Bob was asleep – but the tabby cat wasn't. She was uneasy, but she didn't know why. Her ash tree began to swing and sway rather alarmingly. The tabby was afraid.

Then there came a loud creaking noise. The little cat sprang from her hole in fright. The tree was going to fall! It was, it was! Once before in the wood the tabby had seen a tree blown down in the wind, and had heard the creaking that came before the crash.

The cat stood on a branch and looked towards Bob's house. The ash tree was being blown towards it. Suppose it fell! It would fall right on to Bob's bedroom! He would be hurt and frightened!

The tabby sprang from the creaking, swaying tree and ran to the house. She climbed up the creeper swiftly and came to Bob's window. She slipped inside and jumped on to the sleeping boy's bed.

"Miaow!" she said loudly, and put her whiskery head close against his face. "Miaow!"

She licked him with her rough little tongue and he awoke with a jump. He sat up, astonished.

"Why, it's you, little tabby! Why have you come to see me in the middle of the night? My word, what a wind! What's that creaking noise?"

He went to the window, and saw the great ash tree swaying alarmingly in the gale. It creaked even more loudly – it swayed towards the house – it fell!

Bob gave a shriek! "It's going to fall on the house! Mother! Daddy! Quick!"

He picked up the cat and rushed into his parent's bedroom. Just as he got there, there came a loud crash, and a noise of tiles clattering to the ground. The ash tree had fallen on the house, and had smashed in the roof of Bob's jutting-out bedroom! Tiles fell on to his empty bed, and a great dust filled the room.

“Bob! Darling Bob! You are safe!” cried his mother. “Oh, my dear, thank goodness you woke up in time! You might have been killed.”

“I didn’t wake myself up; the tabby woke me, Mother,” said Bob. “She sleeps in that tree, you know. She must have known it was going to fall and came to warn me. She saved my life, Mother.”

“Good little tabby,” said his mother, and picked up the surprised little cat. “Well, you shall have a reward. You shall be *our* cat now, not a stray any longer. You shall be Bob’s own pet, and he will love you and give you a basket of your own.”

You should have heard the tabby purr! She hadn’t expected any reward at all – but this was the best she could ever have thought of! She jumped up on to Bob’s knee and rubbed her head against him.

"You'd better cuddle into bed with us tonight," said his mother to Bob. "Your bedroom won't be safe till the roof is mended."

So Bob cuddled into his mother's bed – and, dear me, the tabby slept on top of them both. I don't know which was happier, she or Bob?

ISBN 0 00 123752 7

from *Tales After Supper*

Printed in Great Britain